Funny FiLL-IN
MY FLYING ADVENTURE

NATIONAL GEOGRAPHIC
WASHINGTON, D.C.

How to Play Funny Fill-In!

Love to create amazing stories? Good, because this one stars YOU. Get ready to laugh with all your friends—you can play with as many people as you want! Make sure to keep this book on your shelf. You'll want to read it again and again!

Are You Ready to Laugh?

- One person picks a story—you can start at the beginning, the middle, or the end of the book.

- Ask a friend to call out a word that the space asks for—noun, verb, or something else—and write it in the blank space. If there's more than one player, ask the next person to say a word. Extra points for creativity!

- When all the spaces are filled in, you have your very own Funny Fill-In. Read it out loud for a laugh.

- Want to play by yourself? Just fold over the page and use the cardboard insert at the back as a writing pad. Fill in the blank parts of speech list, and copy your answers into the story.

Make sure you check out the amazing **Fun Facts** that appear on every page!

Parts of Speech

To play the game, you'll need to know how to form sentences. This list with examples of the parts of speech and other terms will help you get started:

Noun: The name of a person, place, thing, or idea
Examples: tree, mouth, creature
*The **ocean** is full of colorful **fish**.*

Adjective: A word that describes a noun or pronoun
Examples: green, lazy, friendly
*My **silly** dog won't stop laughing!*

Verb: An action word. In the present tense, a verb often ends in –s or –ing. If the space asks for past tense, changing the vowel or adding a –d or –ed to the end usually will set the sentence in the past.
Examples: swim, hide, plays, running (present tense); biked, rode, jumped (past tense)
*The giraffe **skips** across the savanna.*
*The flower **opened** after the rain.*

Adverb: A word that describes a verb and usually ends in –ly
Examples: quickly, lazily, soundlessly
*Kelley **greedily** ate all the carrots.*

Plural: More than one
Examples: mice, telephones, wrenches
*Why are all the **doors** closing?*

Silly Word or Exclamation: A funny sound, a made-up word, a word you think is totally weird, or a noise someone or something might make
Examples: Ouch! No way! Foozleduzzle! Yikes!
*"**Darn!**" shouted Jim. "These cupcakes are sour!"*

Specific Words: There are many more ways to make your story hilarious. When asked for something like a number, animal, or body part, write in something you think is especially funny.

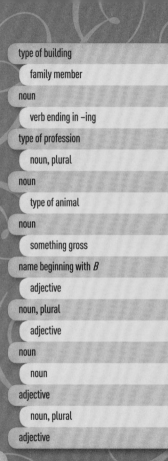

- type of building
- family member
- noun
- verb ending in –ing
- type of profession
- noun, plural
- noun
- type of animal
- noun
- something gross
- name beginning with *B*
- adjective
- noun, plural
- adjective
- noun
- noun
- adjective
- noun, plural
- adjective

Fun Fact! In 2009 in Ishikawa, Japan, citizens reported that it rained tadpoles!

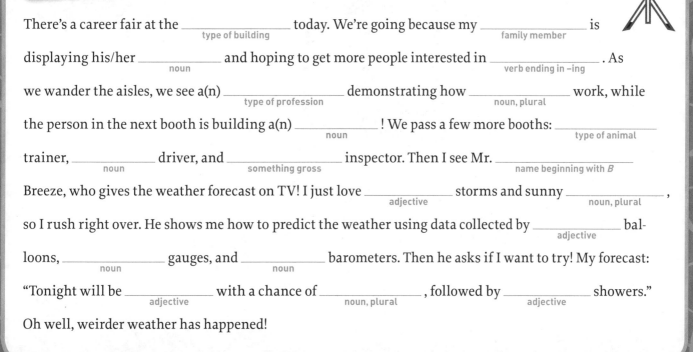

It's a **Breeze**

There's a career fair at the _____ today. We're going because my _____ is

(type of building)   (family member)

displaying his/her _____ and hoping to get more people interested in _____ . As

(noun)   (verb ending in –ing)

we wander the aisles, we see a(n) _____ demonstrating how _____ work, while

(type of profession)   (noun, plural)

the person in the next booth is building a(n) _____ ! We pass a few more booths: _____

(noun)   (type of animal)

trainer, _____ driver, and _____ inspector. Then I see Mr. _____

(noun)   (something gross)   (name beginning with *B*)

Breeze, who gives the weather forecast on TV! I just love _____ storms and sunny _____ ,

(adjective)   (noun, plural)

so I rush right over. He shows me how to predict the weather using data collected by _____ bal-

(adjective)

loons, _____ gauges, and _____ barometers. Then he asks if I want to try! My forecast:

(noun)   (noun)

"Tonight will be _____ with a chance of _____ , followed by _____ showers."

(adjective)   (noun, plural)   (adjective)

Oh well, weirder weather has happened!

5

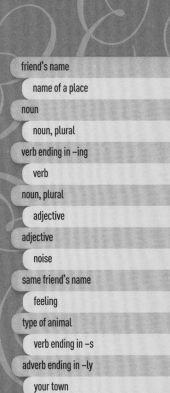

- friend's name
- name of a place
- noun
- noun, plural
- verb ending in –ing
- verb
- noun, plural
- adjective
- adjective
- noise
- same friend's name
- feeling
- type of animal
- verb ending in –s
- adverb ending in –ly
- your town
- adjective

Fun Fact! Weather radios turn on all by themselves when there is an emergency weather warning.

Wacky Weather Warning

_____ is sleeping over at my house tonight. We watch my favorite movie, _The Wizard_
_{friend's name}

_of_ _____ , and play my favorite video game, _____ Fliers. We build airplanes out of
_{name of a place}   _{noun}

_____ and take turns _____ . Then we go out into the backyard and _____
_{noun, plural}   _{verb ending in –ing}   _{verb}

with a kite until the _____ come out. When it gets _____ out, Mom says it's time for
_{noun, plural}   _{adjective}

bed, so we go inside. Just then, we hear a(n) _____ _____ and see a flash of lightning.
_{adjective}   _{noise}

A thunderstorm! _____ is _____ about storms, and even my pet _____
_{same friend's name}   _{feeling}   _{type of animal}

_____ and hides under the bed. Just as we're about to drift off to sleep, my
_{verb ending in –s}

weather radio turns on _____ . "Warning. There is a tornado warning
_{adverb ending in –ly}

for _____ . We're expecting _____ wind ... "
_{your town}   _{adjective}

- adjective ending in –est
  - noun
- noun
  - verb ending in –ed
- noun
  - exclamation
- feeling
  - friend's name
- verb ending in –ing
  - verb ending in –ing
- noun
  - body part
- noun, plural
  - favorite cartoon character
- verb
  - noun
- type of animal
  - noun, plural
- noun, plural

On average, tornadoes last about ten minutes.

Tornado Trouble

I just had the _____ dream! I dreamed I was on a(n) _____ that was twirling like
adjective ending in –est   noun

a(n) _____ , and then I _____ through an open _____ . _____ , was
noun   verb ending in –ed   noun   exclamation

I _____ after that! But when I open my eyes, I see _____ _____ on the
feeling   friend's name   verb ending in –ing

floor—still asleep. My pet is _____ like it has a(n) _____ on its _____ ,
verb ending in –ing   noun   body part

and my toy _____ are flying around my bedroom as though they're real! But it's not until I see
noun, plural

my stuffed _____ _____ across the room and crash into my _____
favorite cartoon character   verb   noun

collection that I figure out what's going on. Sure enough, I look out my window and see a(n) _____
type of animal

fly by! When I look down, there's nothing but _____ for as far as the eye can see. We must
noun, plural

be hundreds of _____ from the ground. My house is caught in a tornado!
noun, plural

9

friend's name

noun

noun, plural

silly word

same friend's name

body part

adjective

color

something fluffy, plural

noun

noun

noun, plural

adjective

noun

adjective

noun

adverb ending in –ly

clothing item, plural

Fun Fact! The "eye," or middle, of a tornado is perfectly calm, but the winds around it can move at speeds of up to 300 miles an hour (483 km/h)!

_____ wakes up, but when I explain what is happening, he/she doesn't believe me at first. Then a
　　friend's name

garden _____ and some _____ fly by the window. "_____!" _____
　　　　　noun　　　　　　　　　　　noun, plural　　　　　　　　　　　　　silly word　　　　　same friend's name

says. Suddenly we get to the _____ of the tornado and everything is eerily _____ .
　　　　　　　　　　　　　　　　body part　　　　　　　　　　　　　　　　　　　　　　adjective

There is a thick wall of fast-moving _____ _____ all around us, but it's as calm
　　　　　　　　　　　　　　　　　　　　　color　　　　something fluffy, plural

as a(n) _____ where we are. From the window we watch a(n) _____ fly by, with some
　　　　　noun　　　　　　　　　　　　　　　　　　　　　　　　　　　　noun

_____ stuck to it. Then a(n) _____ _____ floats by. We're getting
　noun, plural　　　　　　　　　　　　　adjective　　　　　noun

really _____ about seeing a(n) _____ , when suddenly we start to drop
　　　adjective　　　　　　　　　　　　　　noun

_____ . Everyone hold on to your _____ !
adverb ending in –ly　　　　　　　　　　clothing item, plural

noise

   adjective

noun

   adjective

adjective

   noun

verb ending in –ing

   verb ending in –ing

number

   verb

noun

   verb

verb

   type of animal

friend's name

   type of animal

verb

   type of bird

Fun Fact! Wingsuits have webbing under the wearer's arms and between the legs, allowing humans to soar like flying squirrels!

Our house lands with a(n) _____ on a(n) _____ cliff. At first we don't know what to do,
                              noise   adjective

but then we hear a knock on the _____ . When we open the door, a(n) _____ man
                                       noun   adjective

with a(n) _____ beard as long as a(n) _____ is _____ there. He tells us he's
              adjective   noun   verb ending in –ing

been _____ on this cliff for _____ year(s), trying to figure out how to _____ like
     verb ending in –ing   number   verb

a(n) _____ . When he saw us _____ out of the sky, he knew it was a sign he should return
          noun   verb

to his home. He wishes us well and starts to _____ down the cliff. Easy for him to do; he is as
                                                   verb

nimble as a(n) _____ . But how will we get down? That's when _____ finds
                type of animal   friend's name

the flying _____ suits that the man left behind. So we suit up and _____ toward
            type of animal   verb

the edge of the cliff. Time to soar like a majestic _____ !
                                                      type of bird

- adjective
  - friend's name
- verb ending in –s
  - same verb without –s
- something heavy
  - adjective
- verb
  - body part, plural
- same friend's name
  - verb ending in –ing
- something loud
  - type of animal, plural
- body part, plural
  - body part, plural
- type of animal
  - direction
- direction

 Fun Fact! Birds evolved from feathered dinosaurs, but those dinosaurs couldn't fly!

"_____ luck," _____ says, then _____ off the cliff.
 adjective   _friend's name_   _verb ending in –s_

Nothing else to do but follow, I think, and _____ too. At first I drop like a(n) _____ .
                                              same verb without –s   _something heavy_

"I'm too _____ to _____ !" I cry. I try flapping my _____ , but that just
          adjective   _verb_   _body part, plural_

makes it worse. _____ is _____ like a(n) _____ next to me. Then
                 same friend's name   _verb ending in –ing_   _something loud_

we see a flock of _____ soaring below us. We watch them for a few moments as they tilt
                   type of animal, plural

their _____ from side to side. We straighten our arms, and stretch our _____
       body part, plural   _body part, plural_

out wide, trying to copy them. Soon we're flying like a(n) _____ . But we must be too good
                                                            type of animal

at it, because next thing we know, we're going _____ and _____ instead of down.
                                                direction   _direction_

Up, up, and away!

adjective

    type of flying insect, plural

verb

    noun, plural

body part, plural

    noun

noun

    verb ending in –ing

adjective

    your age

verb ending in –ing

    noun, plural

verb

    body part, plural

name of a superhero

Fun Fact!

Famous artist Leonardo da Vinci drew designs for a flying machine called an ornithopter more than 300 years before the first manned flig

What Goes Up ...

Up ahead we see what looks like _____ _____, so we _____
                                  adjective   type of flying insect, plural   verb

toward them. But when we get up close, we discover that they're actually people in flying machines with

wings shaped like _____. One has wings attached to his _____, while
                   noun, plural   body part, plural

another is sitting on a(n) _____ with wings attached to it. A third is lying on a(n) _____,
                           noun   noun

madly _____ a crank to keep a pair of wings moving. When I ask him why he looks so
       verb ending in –ing

_____, the man says, "We were so busy inventing flying machines, we forgot to think of a way
 adjective

to get down! We've been up here for _____ years!" We tell them to try _____ their
                                     your age   verb ending in –ing

_____, then _____ their _____. It works! They look at us like
 noun, plural   verb   body part, plural

we're _____ and head down to the ground. Now if only we could get down too!
       name of a superhero

greeting

famous heroine

type of pet, plural

adjective

adjective

adjective ending in –est

noun

adjective

silly word

noun

name of a city

adjective

your teacher's name

verb

noun

verb

Fun Fact! The first hot-air balloon passengers were a duck, a sheep, and a rooster in France in 1783.

Full of Hot Air

"_____!" we hear someone say from beside us. A woman who looks just like _____
　　　　greeting　　　　　　　　　　　　　　　　　　　　　　　　　　　　　　　　　　　　famous heroine

floats by in a hot-air balloon. The basket is filled with _____! It looks _____, so we ask her
　　　　　　　　　　　　　　　　　　　　　　　type of pet, plural　　　　　　　adjective

for a little help. After we crawl into the _____ basket, we take the _____ trip of our
　　　　　　　　　　　　　　　　　　adjective　　　　　　　　　　adjective ending in –est

lives. We float over the _____ River and some _____ valleys. We pass the _____
　　　　　　　　　　　noun　　　　　　　　　　　　adjective　　　　　　　　　　　　silly word

spire of the famous _____ building in _____. Then I see the _____ peaks
　　　　　　　　　noun　　　　　　　　　name of a city　　　　　　　　adjective

of Mount _____. We're headed straight for it! The woman turns to us and says, "Sorry, but
　　　　your teacher's name

I need to lighten some weight from the basket or I'll never _____ over that _____-shaped
　　　　　　　　　　　　　　　　　　　　　　　　　　　　　verb　　　　　　　　　noun

peak." She hands us some parachutes and tells us to _____. What else can we do?
　　　　　　　　　　　　　　　　　　　　　　　　　　verb

We strap them on and take a leap! Look out below!

noun

> body part

noun

> friend's name

dance move

> gymnastics move

relative's name

> body part, plural

color

> clothing item

verb

> number

geometric shape

> type of dessert

same friend's name

> body part

number

Fun Fact! In 2006, 400 skydivers jumped out of five planes to link together in a record-breaking formation while free-falling!

The _____ is rushing past my _____ , and I feel like I'm dropping faster than
     noun   _body part_

a(n) _____ when I see _____ doing the _____ and a(n) _____
     noun   _friend's name_   _dance move_   _gymnastics move_

while skydiving. He/she looks like _____ at a concert. Just as I'm wondering if it's time to
                                     relative's name

pull my rip cord, someone grabs my _____ . It's another skydiver in a _____ _____
                           body part, plural   _color_   _clothing item_

who starts to _____ . Then _____ other skydiver(s) appear(s) and begin to make a(n) _____
       verb   _number_   _geometric shape_

formation. But the next formation is really complicated: It looks just like a(n) _____ , with
                                           type of dessert

_____ right at the center of it all! Amazing! The skydivers give us a(n) _____'s up
same friend's name   _body part_

and wave goodbye. I high-_____ my friend—the star of the show!
              number

feeling

> verb

verb

> something squishy

something that smells good, plural

> friend's name

verb ending in –ing

> adjective

noun

> piece of furniture, plural

adjective

> noun, plural

same friend's name

> adjective

verb

> body part

type of animal

Fun Fact! Some scientists think that storm clouds on Saturn and Jupiter produce diamonds instead of hail!

Sky-cation

We're starting to get a little _____ from all the flying, so we _____ to a nearby cloud for a
                                    feeling   *verb*

rest. At first, it's hard to _____ on the clouds. It's like wading through piles of _____ .
                              verb   *something squishy*

But it sort of smells like _____ . I think I've lost _____ , but then I see
                            something that smells good, plural   *friend's name*

him/her _____ in a(n) _____ cloud _____ . That's the right idea! We build
        verb ending in –ing   *adjective*   *noun*

ourselves some cloud _____ and hang over the edge, watching the world below. The
                           piece of furniture, plural

people on the ground look like _____ _____ from way up here. _____
                             adjective   *noun, plural*   *same friend's name*

offers me a(n) _____ cloud smoothie, then we decide to _____ in the clouds.
                  adjective   *verb*

Next I practice my _____-stroke and my _____-paddle. Aah, this
                        body part   *type of animal*

is the life!

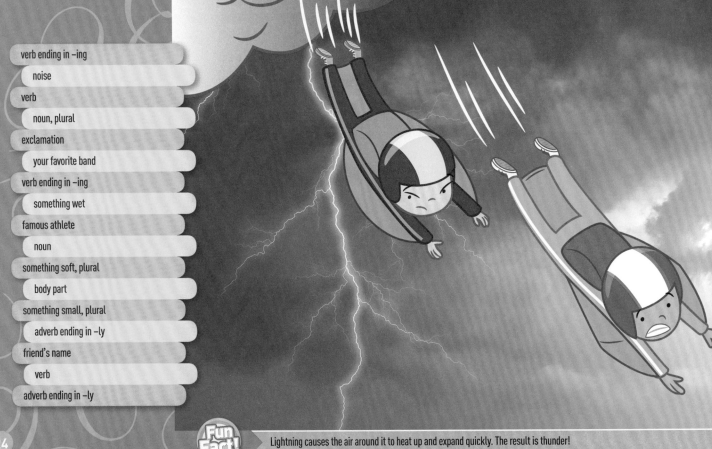

verb ending in –ing

noise

verb

noun, plural

exclamation

your favorite band

verb ending in –ing

something wet

famous athlete

noun

something soft, plural

body part

something small, plural

adverb ending in –ly

friend's name

verb

adverb ending in –ly

24

Fun Fact!

Lightning causes the air around it to heat up and expand quickly. The result is thunder!

Thunder Rumble

We're _____ on a cloud when suddenly we hear a loud _____ and the cloud starts
         verb ending in –ing   _noise_

to _____ . We hang on for our dear _____ ! There's a flash of light below us. _____ ,
     verb   _noun, plural_   _exclamation_

who else is in the cloud? Is it _____ playing their new song, "_____ in
                                 your favorite band   _verb ending in –ing_

the _____ "? Or maybe _____ throwing around a(n) _____ ? I'm so
     something wet   _famous athlete_   _noun_

excited, all of the _____ on my _____ are standing straight up! But then the
                     something soft, plural   _body part_

cloud lights up again and a rush of hot air knocks us down like we're _____ ! Ow!
                                                                        something small, plural

We must be on a storm cloud! We'd better get off—_____ ! But the only way off
                                                    adverb ending in –ly

is down, so _____ and I _____ as _____ as we can,
             friend's name   _verb_   _adverb ending in –ly_

then dive in!

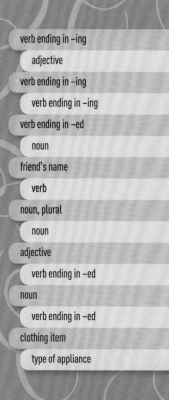

- verb ending in –ing
- adjective
- verb ending in –ing
- verb ending in –ing
- verb ending in –ed
- noun
- friend's name
- verb
- noun, plural
- noun
- adjective
- verb ending in –ed
- noun
- verb ending in –ed
- clothing item
- type of appliance

Fun Fact! Hurricanes and tropical storms are given names so that forecasters can tell them apart when more than one occurs at a time.

We're _____ through the clouds, but they go on forever! We're completely _____ .
verb ending in –ing adjective

I'd rather be home _____ or _____ than here. But the worst is yet to come. Suddenly
verb ending in –ing verb ending in –ing

we're being blasted by hot- and cold-air currents. We're in a hurricane! I feel like I'm being _____
verb ending in –ed

around in a(n) _____ . _____ and I _____ our way toward the eye of the storm,
noun friend's name verb

where the _____ will be calmer. We stay on the edge—we don't want to fall into the _____ .
noun, plural noun

Below us, we see ocean waves that are _____ ! There's a ship down there, being _____
adjective verb ending in –ed

around like a(n) _____ . I hope we get out of this storm soon. I'm being _____ like I'm
noun verb ending in –ed

a(n) _____ being tossed around in a(n) _____ !
clothing item type of appliance

verb

noun

verb

large number

type of insect, plural

number

verb

celebrity's name

adjective ending in –er

verb

adjective

body part

girl's name beginning with *W*

clothing item

something fluffy, plural

friend's name

something shiny, plural

Fun Fact! Starting in the 1920s, wing walkers performed all sorts of crazy tricks, such as doing a handstand on the wings of a flying plane!

Wonderful Wing Walkers

We see land at last! I'm so relieved I could _____ a(n) _____ ! We
                                        verb   noun

start to fall, and I _____ for my parachute. Suddenly I hear a sound like _____ buzzing
                       verb   large number

_____ and see a plane with _____ wing(s) on each side. We _____ and land in the
type of insect, plural   number   verb

plane. "You're just in time!" the pilot says. She looks like _____ , only _____ .
                                                              celebrity's name   adjective ending in –er

She hands us some paper flyers and tells us we're going to _____ them. Then the plane dives over
                                                             verb

a(n) _____ town. "Drop 'em!" the pilot commands, and we throw the flyers out. One flies back
        adjective

onto my _____ . It says, "Wild _____'s Wonderful Wing Walkers! No Wires!"
          body part   girl's name beginning with W

The pilot hands me a(n) _____ with _____ on it and gives _____
                          clothing item   something fluffy, plural   friend's name

a tutu covered in _____ . Is she expecting us to be the stars of the show?
                    something shiny, plural

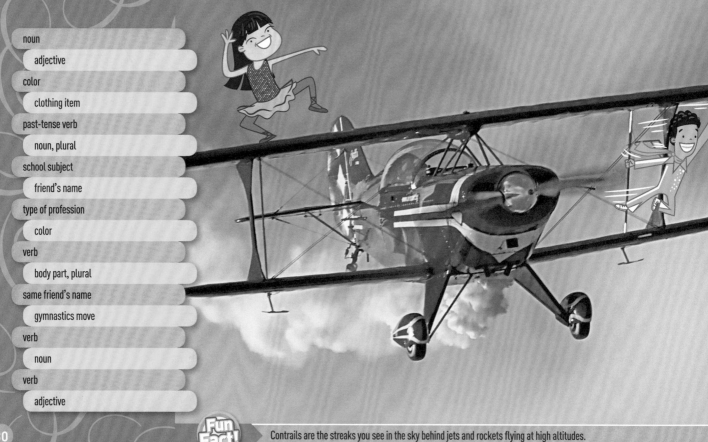

- noun
  - adjective
- color
  - clothing item
- past-tense verb
  - noun, plural
- school subject
  - friend's name
- type of profession
  - color
- verb
  - body part, plural
- same friend's name
  - gymnastics move
- verb
  - noun
- verb
  - adjective

Fun Fact! Contrails are the streaks you see in the sky behind jets and rockets flying at high altitudes.

Famed Fliers

I'm on the _____ of a plane, dressed in a(n) _____ _____ _____. How did
     noun   _adjective_   _color_   _clothing item_

I get myself into this? As if it's not embarrassing enough to be the kid who accidentally _____
                                                                                                                past-tense verb

their _____ in the _____ room! _____ wants to be a(n) _____
         noun, plural   _school subject_   _friend's name_   _type of profession_

and thinks hanging from a biplane by your teeth in a fancy, sparkly _____ tutu is fun! For our first act,
                                                                                                color

we _____ our _____ and wave at the crowd below. Then _____ does
     verb   _body part, plural_   _same friend's name_

a(n) _____ while I _____. We finish off with a spectacular _____ formation.
       gymnastics move   _verb_   _noun_

The people below _____ like crazy. But then we pass through some clouds and see what looks like
                            verb

a(n) _____ jet. My friend and I shrug and decide to jump on it at the same time. Our fans on the
       adjective

ground all cheer and wave goodbye.

animal noise ending in –ing

adjective

color

noun

verb

friend's name

adjective

verb

type of profession, plural

something soft

verb ending in –ing

verb ending in –ing

type of bird

electronic gadget

verb ending in –ing

exotic location

adjective

verb

Fun Fact! The arctic tern migrates 44,000 miles (70,800 km) round-trip from Pole to Pole—farther than any other animal!

Migration Madness

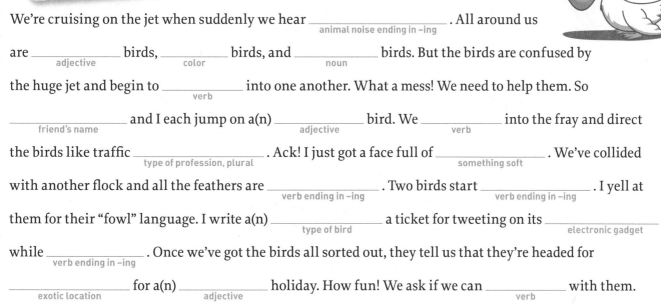

We're cruising on the jet when suddenly we hear _____ . All around us
(animal noise ending in –ing)

are _____ birds, _____ birds, and _____ birds. But the birds are confused by
(adjective)   (color)   (noun)

the huge jet and begin to _____ into one another. What a mess! We need to help them. So
(verb)

_____ and I each jump on a(n) _____ bird. We _____ into the fray and direct
(friend's name)   (adjective)   (verb)

the birds like traffic _____ . Ack! I just got a face full of _____ . We've collided
(type of profession, plural)   (something soft)

with another flock and all the feathers are _____ . Two birds start _____ . I yell at
(verb ending in –ing)   (verb ending in –ing)

them for their "fowl" language. I write a(n) _____ a ticket for tweeting on its _____
(type of bird)   (electronic gadget)

while _____ . Once we've got the birds all sorted out, they tell us that they're headed for
(verb ending in –ing)

_____ for a(n) _____ holiday. How fun! We ask if we can _____ with them.
(exotic location)   (adjective)   (verb)

verb

   letter of the alphabet

part of a bird

   adjective

verb ending in –ing

   verb

noun, plural

   type of animal

verb

   friend's name

same friend's name

   adjective

verb

   type of transportation

silly word

   animal noise

Fun Fact! Birds fly in a V-formation to save energy by using the airflow of the bird in front of them.

Most birds _____ in a V-formation, but our birds have moved into a(n) _____ -formation.
                 verb   letter of the alphabet

My bird, which I have named _____ -foot the _____ , is leading the flock. He says he's
                                part of a bird   adjective

looking forward to _____ this winter. I tell him I like to _____ _____
                      verb ending in –ing   verb   noun, plural

when I'm on vacation. He starts to get tired—and no wonder, I weigh as much as a(n) _____ !
                                                                                          type of animal

We _____ to the back of the formation and _____ 's bird moves to the front. Only,
      verb   friend's name

_____ insists on giving his/her bird directions. We go too low, and get lost in a(n) _____
   same friend's name   adjective

fog. Then we _____ , but we go too high and get caught in the _____ stream. _____ ,
                  verb   type of transportation   silly word

we're really flying off course now! Our bird friends _____ at us.
                                                          animal noise

I think it's time to find a new ride!

- adjective
  - large animal
- verb ending in –s
  - adjective
- verb ending in –ing
  - verb ending in –s
- verb
  - type of food
- adjective
  - type of athlete
- something thin
  - something cute
- verb ending in –s
  - noun
- noun

CLOUD CIRCUS

 Fun Fact! In 1877, 14-year-old Rossa Matilda Richter became the first human cannonball!

Cloud Circus

The birds drop us off on some _____-looking clouds. One of them looks just like a(n) _____!
adjective large animal

It even _____ like one! Another looks like a(n) _____ pony, _____ in the sky.
verb ending in –s adjective verb ending in –ing

Then it _____! I always knew cloud animals were real! We play a quick game of _____-the-
verb ending in –s verb

animal with our new cloud friends. Then we smell _____ and hear a voice calling, "Come one, come
type of food

all to the Cloud Circus! Meet the _____ lady, see our _____ perform death-defying tricks
adjective type of athlete

on a(n) _____ suspended from high above!" We buy tickets and the show is awesome, though the
something thin

cloud _____ really freaks me out when it _____ a(n) _____! The best part of
something cute verb ending in –s noun

the show is when they shoot a(n) _____ out of a cloud cannon!
noun

large number

verb

your town

noun

noun

adjective

verb

body part, plural

body part, plural

weather phenomenon, plural

adjective

verb

noun, plural

noun, plural

friend's name

adjective

adjective

38

Fun Fact! The sound of a balloon popping is actually a small sonic boom!

Balloon Busters

We leave the Cloud Circus with _____ balloons so we can _____ around looking
                                 large number   verb

for _____ . If we see the _____ or the _____ , we'll know we're almost
      your town   noun   noun

there. Suddenly, I see a(n) _____ cloud heading for us. Not again! We try to _____
                               adjective   verb

the balloons in the opposite direction. I frantically try flapping my _____ and kicking
                                                                      body part, plural

my _____ . It doesn't work. I hear a buzzing sound. More _____ ? No, it's
     body part, plural   weather phenomenon, plural

bees! Giant _____ bees! We're afraid to _____ , so we stay as still as _____ as they
               adjective   verb   noun, plural

pop our balloons with stingers as sharp as _____ . "We will take you to our queen," one says.
                                             noun, plural

"Oh, does she have honey?" I say. _____ looks at me like I'm _____ . Well, I'm hungry!
                                   friend's name   adjective

It's been a(n) _____ day!
                 adjective

adjective

    body part, plural

type of animal

    verb

noun, plural

    adjective

noun, plural

    something shiny

verb

    adverb ending in –ly

friend's name

    body part

verb

    same friend's name

verb ending in –ing

    adjective

type of structure

    noise

40

Fun Fact! Drones come in all shapes and sizes and have many uses, including surveillance, hurricane research, disaster recovery, and filmmaking.

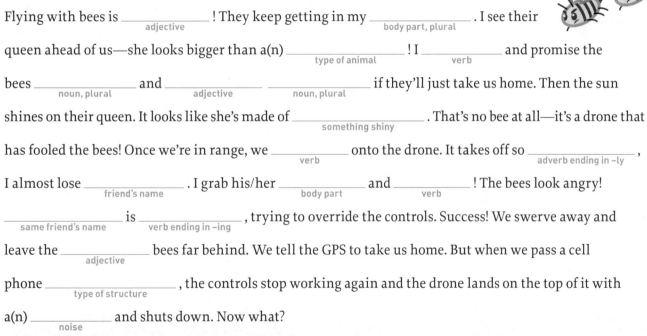

Flying with bees is _____ ! They keep getting in my _____ . I see their
                    adjective   body part, plural

queen ahead of us—she looks bigger than a(n) _____ ! I _____ and promise the
                                              type of animal   verb

bees _____ and _____ _____ if they'll just take us home. Then the sun
     noun, plural   adjective   noun, plural

shines on their queen. It looks like she's made of _____ . That's no bee at all—it's a drone that
                                                   something shiny

has fooled the bees! Once we're in range, we _____ onto the drone. It takes off so _____ ,
                                             verb   adverb ending in –ly

I almost lose _____ . I grab his/her _____ and _____ ! The bees look angry!
              friend's name   body part   verb

_____ is _____ , trying to override the controls. Success! We swerve away and
same friend's name   verb ending in –ing

leave the _____ bees far behind. We tell the GPS to take us home. But when we pass a cell
          adjective

phone _____ , the controls stop working again and the drone lands on the top of it with
      type of structure

a(n) _____ and shuts down. Now what?
     noise

- verb ending in –ing
- verb
- musical instrument
- clothing item
- your favorite song
- noun
- verb
- something sharp, plural
- exclamation
- adjective ending in –est
- noun
- adjective
- noun, plural
- friend's name
- same musical instrument
- nursery rhyme
- adjective ending in –est

After intense solar storms, the aurora borealis, or northern lights, can be seen far away from the North Pole—even from Florida, U.S.A.!

Singing for the Birds

The sun is _____ , so we decide to _____ from our perch. I pull my _____
_{verb ending in –ing} _{verb} _{musical instrument}

out of my _____ , and we sing our favorite campfire songs, "_____"
_{clothing item} _{your favorite song}

and "Look at the _____ and _____ ." Suddenly, I feel _____ dig into my
_{noun} _{verb} _{something sharp, plural}

shoulders. _____ ! Something's carrying us away. I look up and see the _____
_{exclamation} _{adjective ending in –est}

eagle ever! It drops us in a straw _____ with its eaglets, covers us with a(n) _____
_{noun} _{adjective}

blanket made from _____ , and flies off again. _____ and I blink at each other,
_{noun, plural} _{friend's name}

then shrug. I reach for my _____ , and we start singing "_____ ."
_{same musical instrument} _{nursery rhyme}

The eaglets join in! As if it couldn't get any better, we see the northern lights! The

dancing lights are the _____ thing I've seen! This is the best night ever!
_{adjective ending in –est}

silly name

   verb ending in –ing

friend's name

   verb ending in –ed

type of animal, plural

   body part

something slimy

   something gross, plural

type of vegetable, plural

   adjective

noun, plural

   number

toy

   verb

part of a bird

   body part, plural

Fun Fact! The world's largest bird's nest was built by two bald eagles in Florida. It weighed almost 3 tons (2,722 kg)—more than many rhinoceroses!

I wake up in the eagle's nest. _____ (silly name), the eaglet next to me, keeps _____ (verb ending in –ing) the

blankets. And _____ (friend's name) _____ (verb ending in –ed) all night—it was like sleeping beside a bunch of

wild _____ (type of animal, plural)! Next thing I know, I'm being hit in the _____ (body part) by a(n) _____ (something slimy).

It smells like _____ (something gross, plural)! And I thought _____ (type of vegetable, plural) smelled bad! The _____ (adjective)

eagle mother is trying to feed us. She thinks we're her _____ (noun, plural)! I tell her I just need _____ (number)

more minute(s) of sleep. But she picks me up like I'm a(n) _____ (toy) and drops me at the edge of the nest.

I think she wants me to _____ (verb)! Then a(n) _____ (part of a bird) hits my back and I fall out of the nest!

But soon I stretch out my _____ (body part, plural) and begin to soar. My eagle mother looks so proud!

- verb ending in –ing
- noun
- body part, plural
- noun, plural
- verb
- noun, plural
- verb
- your favorite TV show
- loud noise
- noun, plural
- clothing item, plural
- verb
- friend's name
- feeling
- noun, plural
- noun, plural
- same friend's name
- something soft

Fun Fact! Flying was just a dream until the Wright brothers flew the first powered aircraft at Kitty Hawk, North Carolina, U.S.A., in 1903.

Once again, I'm _____ toward the ground, without a safety _____. I start flapping
_{verb ending in –ing} _{noun}

my _____. No luck. I grab some _____ from a tall tree and _____ them
_{body part, plural} _{noun, plural} _{verb}

like _____. I see my life _____ before my eyes, and I actually don't regret any of the time
_{noun, plural} _{verb}

I spent watching _____. _____! I hit the ground. Well, that wasn't as bad as
_{your favorite TV show} _{loud noise}

I thought it would be. I look around and see _____ and dirty _____. That's
_{noun, plural} _{clothing item, plural}

when I hear, "Get off of me!" I _____ and see _____ looking a bit _____.
_{verb} _{friend's name} _{feeling}

Then I realize I'm back in my bedroom and my _____ and _____ are exactly where
_{noun, plural} _{noun, plural}

I left them. "I had the craziest dream!" I say. "And you were there. And—" Whack! _____
_{same friend's name}

laughs and says, "_____ fight!"
_{something soft}

Credits

Cover, Stu99/iStock; 4, Dot Shock/Shutterstock; 6, Photobank.ch/Shutterstock; 8, Sergey Nivens/Shutterstock; 10, Photobank.ch/Shutterstock; 12, Alexander Ishchenko/Shutterstock; 14, Alexander Ishchenko/Shutterstock; 16, Mariusz S. Jurgielewicz/Shutterstock; 18, Sue C./Shutterstock; 20, Rick Neves/Shutterstock; 22, Pavelk/Shutterstock; 24, Nataliia Melnychuk/Shutterstock; 26, Andrey Yurlov/Shutterstock; 28, Adwo/Shutterstock; 30, Dejan Lazarevic/Shutterstock; 32, Imantsu/Shutterstock; 34, Alexey Stiop/Shutterstock; 36, Muratart/Shutterstock; 38, Svetlana Yudina/Shutterstock; 40, Marekuliasz/Shutterstock; 42, Shin Okamoto/Shutterstock; 44, Walter Spina/iStock; 46, Photobank.ch/Shutterstock

Staff for This Book

Ariane Szu-Tu, *Project Editor*
Jim Hiscott, Jr. and Callie Broaddus, *Art Directors*
Kelley Miller, *Senior Photo Editor*
Jennifer MacKinnon, *Writer*
Dan Sipple, *Illustrator*
Paige Towler, *Editorial Assistant*
Sanjida Rashid and Rachel Kenny, *Design Production Assistants*
Michael Cassady, *Rights Clearance Specialist*
Grace Hill, *Managing Editor*
Joan Gossett, *Senior Production Editor*
Lewis R. Bassford, *Production Manager*
Jenn Hoff, *Manager, Production Services*
Susan Borke, *Legal and Business Affairs*

Published by the National Geographic Society

Gary E. Knell, *President and CEO*
John M. Fahey, *Chairman of the Board*
Melina Gerosa Bellows, *Chief Education Officer*
Declan Moore, *Chief Media Officer*
Hector Sierra, *Senior Vice President and General Manager, Book Division*

Senior Management Team, Kids Publishing and Media

Nancy Laties Feresten, *Senior Vice President*
Jennifer Emmett, *Vice President, Editorial Director, Kids Books*
Julie Vosburgh Agnone, *Vice President, Editorial Operations*
Rachel Buchholz, *Editor and Vice President, NG Kids magazine*
Michelle Sullivan, *Vice President, Kids Digital*
Eva Absher-Schantz, *Design Director*
Jay Sumner, *Photo Director*
Hannah August, *Marketing Director*
R. Gary Colbert, *Production Director*

Digital

Anne McCormack, *Director*
Laura Goertzel, Sara Zeglin, *Producers*
Jed Winer, *Special Projects Assistant*
Emma Rigney, *Creative Producer*
Bianca Bowman, *Assistant Producer*
Natalie Jones, *Senior Product Manager*

Editorial, Design, and Production by Plan B Book Packagers

The National Geographic Society is one of the world's largest nonprofit scientific and educational organizations. Founded in 1888 to "increase and diffuse geographic knowledge," the Society's mission is to inspire people to care about the planet. It reaches more than 400 million people worldwide each month through its official journal, *National Geographic*, and other magazines; National Geographic Channel; television documentaries; music; radio; films; books; DVDs; maps; exhibitions; live events; school publishing programs; interactive media; and merchandise. National Geographic has funded more than 10,000 scientific research, conservation, and exploration projects and supports an education program promoting geographic literacy.

For more information, please visit nationalgeographic.com, call 1-800-NGS LINE (647-5463), or write to the following address:

National Geographic Society
1145 17th Street N.W.
Washington, D.C. 20036-4688 U.S.A.

Visit us online at nationalgeographic.com/books

For librarians and teachers: ngchildrensbooks.org

More for kids from National Geographic: kids.nationalgeographic.com

For information about special discounts for bulk purchases, please contact National Geographic Books Special Sales: ngspecsales@ngs.org

For rights or permissions inquiries, please contact National Geographic Books Subsidiary Rights: ngbookrights@ngs.org

ISBN: 978-1-4263-2065-1

Printed in China

15/RRDS/1